brjc
1/12

Reptiles
Eastern Box Turtles

by Elizabeth Thomas

Consulting Editor: Gail Saunders-Smith, PhD

Content Consultant: Tanya Dewey, PhD
University of Michigan Museum of Zoology

CAPSTONE PRESS
a capstone imprint

Pebble Plus is published by Capstone Press,
151 Good Counsel Drive, P.O. Box 669, Mankato, Minnesota 56002.
www.capstonepub.com

 Books published by Capstone Press are manufactured with paper
containing at least 10 percent post-consumer waste.

Library of Congress Cataloging-in-Publication Data
Thomas, Elizabeth, 1953–
 Eastern box turtles / by Elizabeth Thomas.
   p. cm.—(Pebble plus. Reptiles)
 Includes bibliographical references and index.
 Summary: "Simple text and photographs present Eastern Box Turtles, how they look, where they live, and what they
do"—Provided by publisher.
 ISBN 978-1-4296-6643-5 (library binding)
 1. Box turtle—Juvenile literature. I. Title.
 QL666.C547T46 2012
 597.92'5—dc22
                    2011002111

Editorial Credits

Lori Shores, editor; Gene Bentdahl, designer; Laura Manthe, production specialist

Photo Credits

Alamy: Jeff Greenberg, 21, Ryan M. Bolton, 1; CORBIS: David A. Northcott, 11, Visuals Unlimited/Michael Redmer,
9; Dreamstime/Meraleigh, back cover; Getty Images Inc.: Danita Delimont/Gallo Images, front cover, National
Geographic/George Grall, 5; iStockphoto: Nancy Brammer, 7; Shutterstock: Jason Patrick Ross, 13, Ryan M. Bolton, 15;
Super Stock Inc.: Animals Animals, 19

Note to Parents and Teachers

The Reptiles set supports science standards related to life science. This book describes and
illustrates eastern box turtles. The images support early readers in understanding the text. The
repetition of words and phrases helps early readers learn new words. This book also introduces
early readers to subject-specific vocabulary words, which are defined in the Glossary section.
Early readers may need assistance to read some words and to use the Table of Contents,
Glossary, Read More, Internet Sites, and Index sections of the book.

Printed in the United States of America in North Mankato, Minnesota.
032011
006110CGF11

Table of Contents

All Boxed In

Eastern box turtles

get their name

from their shells.

Their shells snap closed

like a box.

Up Close!

Eastern box turtles grow

from 5.5 to 8 inches

(14 to 20 centimeters) long.

Their shells are golden brown

with dark brown patches.

Eastern box turtles

have claws for digging,

but not for fighting enemies.

Their bone-hard shells

keep their soft bodies safe.

Eastern box turtles eat
worms, bugs, fruit,
and vegetables.
They take small bites
with their sharp beaks.

At Home

Eastern box turtles live
in the eastern United States.
They make homes in
leafy woods and
grassy areas.

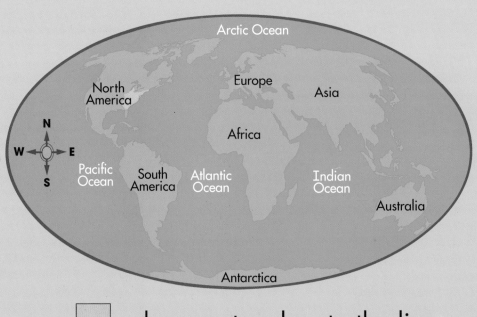

where eastern box turtles live

In winter, an eastern box

turtle hibernates.

It tucks in its legs

and head.

Then it closes its shell.

From Egg to Turtle

Female eastern box turtles
lay three to eight eggs.
They cover the small,
white eggs with dirt.

Eastern Box Turtle Life Cycle

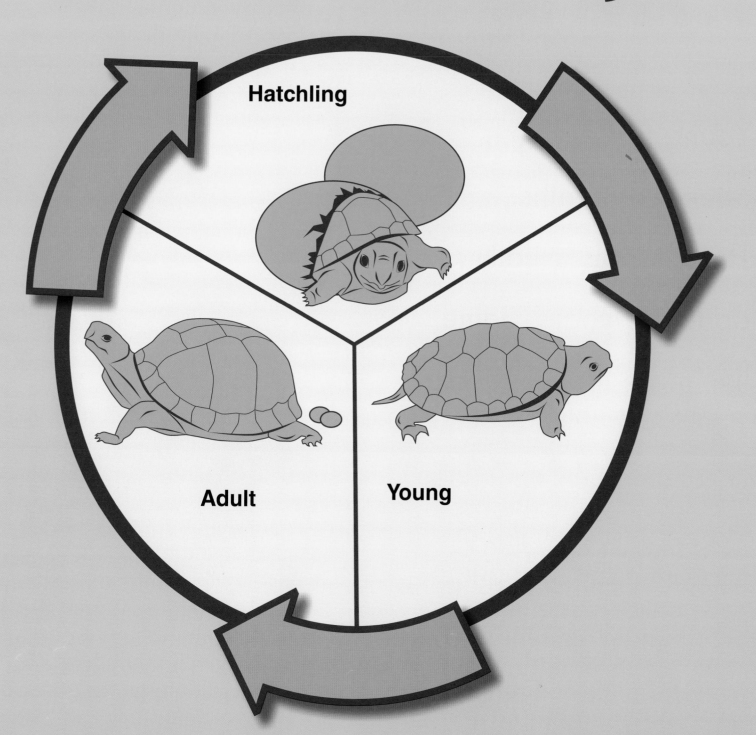

Hatchling

Adult

Young

Young turtles hatch
after two months.
These turtles usually live
about 50 years. Some
live more than 100 years.

Save the Turtles!

Turtles lose their homes
when people build
new roads and houses.
People are working to
protect these turtles' homes.

Glossary

beak—a hard mouthpart on some animals; turtles have beaks instead of teeth

claw—a hard curved nail on the foot of an animal

hatch—to break out of an egg

hibernate—to spend winter in a deep sleep; animals hibernate to survive low temperatures and lack of food

Read More

Bredeson, Carmen. *Fun Facts about Turtles!* I Like Reptiles and Amphibians! Berkeley Heights, N.J.: Enslow Elementary, 2008.

Harris, Tim, editor. *Turtles.* Slimy, Scaly, Deadly Reptiles and Amphibians. New York: Gareth Stevens Pub., 2010.

Randolph, Joanne. *My Friend the Box Turtle.* Curious Pet Pals. New York: Windmill Books, 2010.

Internet Sites

FactHound offers a safe, fun way to find Internet sites related to this book. All of the sites on FactHound have been researched by our staff.

Here's all you do:

Visit *www.facthound.com*

Type in this code: 9781429666435

Super-cool stuff!

Check out projects, games and lots more at
www.capstonekids.com

Index

Word Count: 152

Grade: 1

Early-Intervention Level: J